PRAY UNTIL SOMETHING HAPPENS

HEATHER G. WACHTER

The P.U.S.H. Journal
Copyright © 2016 by Heather G. Wachter
Design by Kelly Bennema

All rights reserved. Without limiting the rights under copyright reserved above, no part of this publication may be reproduced, stored in or introduced into a retrieval system, or transmitted, in any form, or by any means (electronic, mechanical, photocopying, recording, or otherwise) without the prior written permission of the copyright owner of this book.

All scripture quotations, unless otherwise indicated, are taken from the Holy Bible, New International Version®, NIV®. Copyright ©1973, 1978, 1984, 2011 by Biblica, Inc.™ Used by permission of Zondervan. All rights reserved worldwide. http://www.zondervan.com/.

The "NIV" and "New International Version" are trademarks registered in the United States Patent and Trademark Office by Biblica, Inc.™

ISBN: 978-1-365-12305-4

The P.U.S.H. Journal

is dedicated

to my sweet loves,

Johnathan Courage and William Liberty,

God's boldest answers

to my prayers.

Here's a confession: Sometimes I struggle to remember who and what I should pray for. It's embarrassing to admit, but it's true.

We often say or hear others saying, "I'm praying for you." I don't know about you, but when I settle down to pray in quiet moments, I can feel frustrated trying to remember who or what I want – or have committed – to pray for. I'm pretty good at remembering my daily prayers of gratitude for the beautiful life God has granted me, my family, my friends, my good health and stability, and my church. But once I dig deeper in prayer, I often start off well and end weakly, regretting that I've forgotten people and issues important to me.

The P.U.S.H. Journal was designed to help us – you and me, too! – to be more intentional in prayer, to remember to pray for the people we love and the issues we care about, and to follow and celebrate the progress of our prayers, thanks to God.

God wants us to pray to Him. Many times throughout the Bible, He encourages us to come to Him in prayer. Here are just a few instances...

> "If you believe, you will receive whatever you **ask for in prayer**." Matthew 21:22

> "Therefore confess your sins to each other and **pray for** each other so that you may be healed. The prayer of a righteous person is powerful and effective." James 5:16

> "Hear my cry for help, my King and my God, **for to you I pray**." Psalm 5:2

Throughout this journal, you'll find more scripture and also powerful quotes encouraging you to do just this...pray until something happens.

In the Beginning...

The idea of the P.U.S.H. Journal was originally spurred by a conversation with my dear cousin, Leslie. When my brother, David, was serving in the US Navy in Iraq, Leslie asked me to send her a photo of David to include with her prayer list; she said that having photos helped her focus on those for whom she was praying. But what struck me was that she keeps a list of her prayers. She intentionally tracked the loved ones for whom she prayed, rather than relying on her own very human memory. What a great idea!

Shortly after that conversation with Leslie, I drove past a small church in our town that's well known for its thought-provoking marquee postings. The marquee read:

P.U.S.H.
Pray Until Something Happens

It reminded me of forgetful fish Dory's mantra in the Nemo movies, "Just keep swimming...just keep swimming...just keep swimming...," but with a much more practical human application: "Just keep praying...just keep praying...just keep praying..." Dory can't remember much, but she knows to stay focused by doing the most important thing, over and over and over.

I began crafting the idea of a P.U.S.H. Journal as a tool to help me, and ultimately others, to be persistent and focused in prayer...and to see God's work alight in our lives.

What happened next? I prayed about it.

Reading the best-selling novel, <u>The Help</u>, sealed the deal. Learning about Aibileen's faithful daily prayer journaling was as if God himself were telling me, "Yes! You need to create this." I had prayed about it, and there He was, answering my prayers – *He was making something happen,* **in** *me and* **through** *me, in response to my prayers.*

When I journal in my prayer life, I obtain clarity. The people and things I care about get the heartfelt prayers I promise them, the prayers they need, the prayers God is longing to hear and respond to. Most importantly, when I journal in my prayer life, I see God working in beautiful, unimaginable ways. He is most clearly present to me when I am in regular connection with Him through purposeful, ongoing prayer.

So here you have it: The P.U.S.H. Journal. It's here for you to be intentional in prayer; to reflect on your past, your present and your future; to appreciate and nurture your relationships; to delight in life's mysteries; to wrestle with your world's unique challenges. And to watch the glorious hands of God at work in your life, responding to your prayers to Him.

That is my prayer for you.

Using Your P.U.S.H. Journal

It's YOUR journal! So please, use The P.U.S.H. Journal in whatever ways best suit your personal style. It's designed to be a helpful guide, not a restrictive structure.

The P.U.S.H. Journal's pages are mostly blank, with the exception of some inspirational quotes and pieces of scripture, along with the occasional prompt to encourage you on your P.U.S.H. journey.

At the bottom of every other page, you'll find a section asking you, "How is God responding to your prayers?" This is your opportunity to record who and what you're praying for, and – the most exciting part – how you see God responding to your prayers! You can list names, jot brief bullet points, or write descriptive sentences for each area of your prayer life for which you're P.U.S.H.ing. Take note of what people have told you, what actions you've seen, and what results you've experienced. And be sure to record the date so you'll see the progress of your prayer journey over time. Sometimes God responds immediately, and sometimes you'll learn to nurture the Holy Spirit's gift of patience in the process. Stay the course, and watch the glory of God at work as your P.U.S.H. journey unfolds.

If you'd like, you can bookmark, dog-ear or sticky-tab especially notable reflection pages to find and revisit them easily throughout your P.U.S.H. journey.

What if you're new to journaling? Are you unsure of how to approach your P.U.S.H. journey? Here are some ideas:

If you're an artist, you can illustrate your visions of situations you're praying for, what God has revealed to you, and embellishments of the results of your P.U.S.H. as they become clear...

If you're a dreamer, you can jot your thoughts as they come to you, wherever and however you'd like...

If you're an organizer, you can designate a page (or a two-page spread) for each prayer, and detail its progress, chronologically or systematically, as it unfolds...

If you're an evangelist, you can describe God's glory where you see its potential, regale in its splendor as it comes to fruition, and reveal how you're sharing it with others...

If you're a visionary, you can describe your ideas as they take hold, pray for clarity and direction, and follow God's promptings...

If you're a list-maker, you can create your list, and then follow the progression of each item as God makes things happen...

If you pray in response to scripture, you can choose a passage, write it down, pray about it, and reveal in writing what God illuminates for you...

...the beautiful bottom line is...The P.U.S.H. Journal is yours for the making!

Just like my cousin Leslie did, you can use photos or images of your own to help focus your prayers – tape or clip them to pages, tuck them inside the front or back cover, or use them as bookmarks for the various pages and stages in your P.U.S.H. journey.

I pray that you will find new joy in prayer and see God at work in your life as you use The P.U.S.H. Journal!

The Lord's Prayer

One day Jesus was praying in a certain place. When he finished, one of his disciples said to him, "Lord, teach us to pray, just as John taught his disciples."

He said to them, "When you pray, say:

"'Father,
hallowed be your name,
your kingdom come.
Give us each day our daily bread.
Forgive us our sins,
for we also forgive everyone who sins against us.
And lead us not into temptation.'"

Then Jesus said to them, "Suppose you have a friend, and you go to him at midnight and say, 'Friend, lend me three loaves of bread; a friend of mine on a journey has come to me, and I have no food to offer him.' And suppose the one inside answers, 'Don't bother me. The door is already locked, and my children and I are in bed. I can't get up and give you anything.' I tell you, even though he will not get up and give you the bread because of friendship, yet because of your shameless audacity he will surely get up and give you as much as you need.

"So I say to you: Ask and it will be given to you; seek and you will find; knock and the door will be opened to you. For everyone who asks receives; the one who seeks finds; and to the one who knocks, the door will be opened."

LUKE 11:1-10

New International Version (NIV)

A Prayer for You

Dear God,

Thank You for placing The P.U.S.H. Journal into the hands that now hold it. Please make it a useful and encouraging tool for this Beloved Child of Yours, to foster intentional prayer and to reveal Your work in response to those prayers. Bless the writer and those for whom prayers are chronicled. Thank You for Your goodness and Your faithfulness.

Amen.

Grow flowers of gratitude

in the soil of prayer.
— VERBENA WOODS

ever have one of **THOSE DAYS?**

YOU DON'T HAVE TO **PUSH** through it alone.

LEAN ON **GOD** AND HE'LL HELP YOU through.

HOW IS GOD RESPONDING TO YOUR PRAYERS?

I BELIEVE IN *prayer.* IT'S THE BEST WAY WE

HAVE TO DRAW *strength* FROM HEAVEN.
— JOSEPHINE BAKER

> IF YOU REMAIN IN ME AND MY WORDS REMAIN IN YOU, ASK WHATEVER YOU WISH, AND IT WILL BE DONE FOR YOU. — John 15:7

HOW IS GOD RESPONDING TO YOUR PRAYERS?

> PRAYER
> IS COMMUNICATION
> WITH THE DIVINE. IT CAN BE
> WHISPERED OR CHANTED OR
> WRITTEN OR EXPRESSED IN THE WORK
> YOU DO. HOWEVER IT IS EXPRESSED,
> IT IS NEVER IN VAIN.
>
> *Donna Wilk Cardillo*

SO WHAT SHALL I DO? I WILL PRAY WITH MY SPIRIT, BUT I WILL ALSO PRAY WITH MY UNDERSTANDING; I WILL SING WITH MY SPIRIT, BUT I WILL ALSO SING WITH MY UNDERSTANDING.

1 Corinthians 14:15

HOW IS GOD RESPONDING TO YOUR PRAYERS?

> BE NOT FORGETFUL OF PRAYER. EVERY TIME YOU PRAY, IF YOUR PRAYER IS SINCERE, THERE WILL BE A NEW FEELING AND NEW MEANING IN IT, WHICH WILL GIVE YOU FRESH COURAGE, AND YOU WILL UNDERSTAND THAT PRAYER IS AN EDUCATION.
> — Fyodor Dostoyevsky

> ASK AND IT WILL BE GIVEN TO YOU; SEEK AND YOU WILL FIND; KNOCK AND THE DOOR WILL BE OPENED TO YOU. FOR EVERYONE WHO ASKS RECEIVES; THE ONE WHO SEEKS FINDS; AND TO THE ONE WHO KNOCKS, THE DOOR WILL BE OPENED.
> — Matthew 7:7-8

HOW IS GOD RESPONDING TO YOUR PRAYERS?

> BY MY DEFINITION, *prayer* IS CONSCIOUSLY HANGING OUT WITH GOD. BEING WITH GOD IN A *deliberate* WAY.
>
> — Malcolm Boyd

FOR GREAT IS HIS *love* TOWARD US, AND THE *faithfulness* OF THE LORD ENDURES FOREVER. PRAISE THE LORD. — PSALM 117:2

HOW IS GOD RESPONDING TO YOUR PRAYERS?

PRAYER IS *exhaling* THE SPIRIT OF MAN

AND *inhaling* THE SPIRIT OF GOD.
— EDWIN KEITH

> DO NOT BE ANXIOUS ABOUT ANYTHING, BUT IN EVERY SITUATION, BY PRAYER AND PETITION, WITH THANKSGIVING, PRESENT YOUR REQUESTS TO GOD.
> — Philippians 4:6

HOW IS GOD RESPONDING TO YOUR PRAYERS?

What are you P.U.S.H.ing for?

ANY CONCERN TOO SMALL TO BE TURNED INTO A PRAYER IS TOO SMALL TO BE MADE INTO A BURDEN.

— Corrie Ten Boom

HOW IS GOD RESPONDING TO YOUR PRAYERS?

Watch and pray so that you

WILL NOT FALL INTO TEMPTATION.
— MATTHEW 26:41

The Serenity Prayer

God grant me the serenity
to accept the things I cannot change;
courage to change the things I can;
and wisdom to know the difference.
Living one day at a time;
enjoying one moment at a time;
accepting hardships as the pathway to peace;
taking, as He did, this sinful world
as it is, not as I would have it;
trusting that He will make all things right
if I surrender to His Will;
that I may be reasonably happy in this life
and supremely happy with Him
forever in the next.

Amen.

REINHOLD NIEBUHR

HOW IS GOD RESPONDING TO YOUR PRAYERS?

Devote yourselves to prayer,

BEING WATCHFUL AND THANKFUL.

COLOSSIANS 4:2

HOW IS GOD RESPONDING TO YOUR PRAYERS?

> *Anything* large enough for a wish to light upon, is large enough to hang a prayer upon.
> — George MacDonald

> THEREFORE CONFESS YOUR SINS TO EACH OTHER AND PRAY FOR EACH OTHER SO THAT YOU MAY BE HEALED. THE PRAYER OF A RIGHTEOUS PERSON IS POWERFUL AND EFFECTIVE.
>
> — James 5:16

HOW IS GOD RESPONDING TO YOUR PRAYERS?

FAITH AND PRAYER ARE THE *vitamins* OF THE SOUL; MAN CANNOT LIVE IN HEALTH WITHOUT THEM. — MAHALIA JACKSON

God TELLS US TO BURDEN HIM

with whatever BURDENS US.
— AUTHOR UNKNOWN

HOW IS GOD RESPONDING TO YOUR PRAYERS?

SO WE FASTED AND PETITIONED OUR GOD ABOUT THIS, AND HE ANSWERED OUR PRAYER.

— Ezra 8:23

PRAY

FOR THE *people you love* AND THE ISSUES *you care about.*

OBSERVE

THE PROGRESS OF YOUR PRAYERS.

SEE

GOD AT WORK IN YOUR LIFE.

HOW IS GOD RESPONDING TO YOUR PRAYERS?

> IN OUR HOME THERE WAS ALWAYS PRAYER — ALOUD, PROUD AND UNAPOLOGETIC.
>
> — Lyndon B. Johnson

> THEREFORE I TELL YOU, WHATEVER YOU ASK FOR IN PRAYER, BELIEVE THAT YOU HAVE RECEIVED IT, AND IT WILL BE YOURS. — Mark 11:24

HOW IS GOD RESPONDING TO YOUR PRAYERS?

What are you P.U.S.H.ing for?

Prayer REQUIRES MORE OF THE HEART THAN OF THE TONGUE. — ADAM CLARKE

HOW IS GOD RESPONDING TO YOUR PRAYERS?

> PRAYER OPENS THE HEART TO GOD, AND IT IS THE MEANS BY WHICH THE SOUL, THOUGH EMPTY, IS FILLED BY GOD.
>
> John Buchan

I HAVE NOT STOPPED GIVING THANKS FOR YOU.

remembering YOU IN MY PRAYERS.
— EPHESIANS 1:16

HOW IS GOD RESPONDING TO YOUR PRAYERS?

The Peace Prayer

Lord, make me an instrument of your peace.
Where there is hatred, let me sow love,
Where there is injury, pardon;
Where there is doubt, faith,
Where there is despair, hope;
Where there is darkness, light;
Where there is sadness, joy.

O, Divine Master, grant that I may not so much
seek to be consoled as to console;
not so much to be understood as to understand;
not so much to be loved, as to love;
for it is in giving that we receive;
it is in pardoning that we are pardoned;
it is in dying to self that we are born to eternal life.

ST. FRANCIS OF ASSISI

HOW IS GOD RESPONDING TO YOUR PRAYERS?

> PRAYER IS TALKING WITH GOD. GOD KNOWS YOUR HEART AND IS NOT SO CONCERNED WITH YOUR WORDS AS HE IS WITH THE ATTITUDE OF YOUR HEART.
> — Josh McDowell

THE LORD HAS *heard* MY CRY FOR MERCY;

THE LORD *accepts* MY PRAYER.
— Psalm 6:9

HOW IS GOD RESPONDING TO YOUR PRAYERS?

> LET EVERYONE TRY AND FIND THAT AS A RESULT OF DAILY PRAYER HE ADDS SOMETHING NEW TO HIS LIFE, SOMETHING WITH WHICH NOTHING CAN BE COMPARED.
>
> — Mahatma Gandhi

> PRAISE BE TO GOD, WHO HAS NOT REJECTED MY PRAYER OR WITHHELD HIS LOVE FROM ME!
> — Psalm 66:20

HOW IS GOD RESPONDING TO YOUR PRAYERS?

Prayer IS AN EFFORT TO LAY HOLD OF

GOD HIMSELF, THE AUTHOR OF *life*.

— SUNDAR SINGH

> **NOW, MY GOD, MAY YOUR EYES BE OPEN AND YOUR EARS ATTENTIVE TO THE PRAYERS OFFERED IN THIS PLACE.**
>
> — *2 Chronicles 6:40*

HOW IS GOD RESPONDING TO YOUR PRAYERS?

DRAWING A BLANK?

Create a list of **EVERYONE** AND **EVERYTHING** you are *thankful for.*

P.U.S.H. FOR THEM.

WE HAVE TO PRAY WITH OUR *eyes* ON

God, NOT ON THE DIFFICULTIES.
— OSWALD CHAMBERS

HOW IS GOD RESPONDING TO YOUR PRAYERS?

What are you P.U.S.H.ing for?

I ALWAYS thank my God

AS I REMEMBER YOU IN MY PRAYERS...
— Philemon 1:4

HOW IS GOD RESPONDING TO YOUR PRAYERS?

> PRAYER DOES NOT USE UP ARTIFICIAL ENERGY, DOESN'T BURN UP ANY FOSSIL FUEL, DOESN'T POLLUTE. NEITHER DOES SONG, NEITHER DOES LOVE, NEITHER DOES THE DANCE.
>
> — Margaret Mead

> HEAR MY PRAYER, LORD, LISTEN TO MY CRY FOR HELP; DO NOT BE DEAF TO MY WEEPING. I DWELL WITH YOU AS A FOREIGNER, A STRANGER, AS ALL MY ANCESTORS WERE.
> — Psalm 39:12

HOW IS GOD RESPONDING TO YOUR PRAYERS?

Prayer IS MAN'S GREATEST *power!*

— W. CLEMENT STONE

The Irish Blessing

May the road rise to meet you,
May the wind be always at your back,
May the sun shine warm upon your face,
The rains fall soft upon your fields and,
Until we meet again,
May God hold you in the palm of His hand.

ANONYMOUS

HOW IS GOD RESPONDING TO YOUR PRAYERS?

THE SOVEREIGN cure FOR WORRY IS prayer.
— WILLIAM JAMES

HOW IS GOD RESPONDING TO YOUR PRAYERS?

BE *joyful* IN HOPE, *patient* IN

AFFLICTION, *faithful* IN PRAYER.
— Romans 12:12

> HE WHO HAS LEARNED TO PRAY HAS LEARNED THE GREATEST SECRET OF A HOLY AND HAPPY LIFE.
>
> — William Law

HOW IS GOD RESPONDING TO YOUR PRAYERS?

THEN *you* **will call** ON ME AND COME AND PRAY

TO ME, AND I will listen TO YOU.

— JEREMIAH 29:12

> **PRAYER IS NOT SO MUCH THE MEANS WHEREBY GOD'S WILL IS BENT TO MAN'S DESIRES, AS IT IS THAT WHEREBY MAN'S WILL IS BENT TO GOD'S DESIRES.**
>
> *Charles Bent*

HOW IS GOD RESPONDING TO YOUR PRAYERS?

...*bless* THOSE WHO CURSE YOU,

pray FOR THOSE WHO MISTREAT YOU.

— Luke 6:28

YOUR PRAYER IS A
GIFT
TO THOSE FOR
whom you pray.

How
PRECIOUS
is that gift!

HOW IS GOD RESPONDING TO YOUR PRAYERS?

What are you P.U.S.H.ing for?

> HOWEVER ONE MIGHT PRAY — IN ANY VERBAL WAY OR COMPLETELY WITHOUT WORDS — IS UNIMPORTANT TO GOD. WHAT MATTERS IS THE HEART'S INTENT.
>
> — Malcolm Boyd

HOW IS GOD RESPONDING TO
YOUR PRAYERS?

> I CALL ON YOU, MY GOD, FOR YOU WILL ANSWER ME;
> TURN YOUR EAR TO ME AND HEAR MY PRAYER.
>
> — Psalm 17:6

IT IS GOOD FOR US TO KEEP SOME ACCOUNT OF OUR PRAYERS, THAT WE MAY NOT UNSAY THEM IN OUR PRACTICE.

— Matthew Henry

HOW IS GOD RESPONDING TO
YOUR PRAYERS?

LORD, I WAIT FOR YOU;
you will answer,
LORD MY GOD.

PSALM 38:15

> LARGE ASKING AND LARGE EXPECTATION ON OUR PART HONOR GOD.
>
> — A.L. Stone

HOW IS GOD RESPONDING TO
YOUR PRAYERS?

THE LORD IS NEAR TO ALL WHO CALL ON HIM, TO ALL WHO CALL ON HIM IN TRUTH.

Psalm 145:18

Twenty-Third Psalm

The Lord is my shepherd, I lack nothing.
He makes me lie down in green pastures,
he leads me beside quiet waters,
he refreshes my soul.
He guides me along the right paths
for his name's sake.
Even though I walk
through the darkest valley,
I will fear no evil,
for you are with me;
your rod and your staff,
they comfort me.
You prepare a table before me
in the presence of my enemies.
You anoint my head with oil;
my cup overflows.
Surely your goodness and love will follow me
all the days of my life,
and I will dwell in the house of the Lord
forever.

PSALM 23: 1-6

HOW IS GOD RESPONDING TO YOUR PRAYERS?

OF ALL DUTIES, PRAYER CERTAINLY IS THE

sweetest AND MOST EASY.

— LAURENCE STERNE

HOW IS GOD RESPONDING TO YOUR PRAYERS?

Rejoice always, pray *continually*, give thanks in all circumstances...

1 Thessalonians 5:16-18

> **PRAYER DOES NOT CHANGE GOD, BUT IT CHANGES HIM WHO PRAYS.**
> — Søren Kierkegaard

HOW IS GOD RESPONDING TO YOUR PRAYERS?

HEAR MY CRY FOR HELP, MY *King*

AND MY *God*, FOR TO YOU I PRAY.

— Psalm 5:2

THE PURPOSE OF PRAYER IS TO FIND God's will

AND MAKE THAT WILL **our prayer.**
—CATHERINE MARSHALL

HOW IS GOD RESPONDING TO YOUR PRAYERS?

What are you P.U.S.H.ing for?

Think of your prayers as an _intimate conversation_ with **GOD.**

Open your heart to him. Then _listen_ for his **RESPONSE.**

HOW IS GOD RESPONDING TO
YOUR PRAYERS?

An Evening Family Prayer

Lord, behold our family here assembled.
We thank you for this place in which we dwell,
for the love that unites us,
for the peace accorded to us this day,
for the hope with which we expect the morrow;
for the health, the work, the food and the bright skies
that make our lives delightful;
for our friends in all parts of the earth.
Amen.

ROBERT LOUIS STEVENSON

> BUT I CRY TO YOU FOR HELP, LORD; IN THE MORNING MY PRAYER COMES BEFORE YOU.
> — Psalm 88:13

HOW IS GOD RESPONDING TO YOUR PRAYERS?

PRAY AS IF everything

depended ON YOUR PRAYER.

— William Booth

> After Job had prayed for his friends, the Lord restored his fortunes and gave him twice as much as he had before.
>
> Job 42:10

HOW IS GOD RESPONDING TO YOUR PRAYERS?

> IT IS WHEN THE ANSWER TO PRAYER DOES NOT COME...
> THAT THE TRIAL OF FAITH, MORE PRECIOUS THAN GOLD,
> TAKES PLACE.
>
> — Andrew Murray

THE GREAT POINT IS TO *never give*

up UNTIL THE ANSWER COMES.
— George Müller

HOW IS GOD RESPONDING TO YOUR PRAYERS?

> NONE CAN BELIEVE HOW POWERFUL PRAYER IS, AND WHAT IT IS ABLE TO EFFECT, BUT THOSE WHO HAVE LEARNED IT BY EXPERIENCE.
>
> — Martin Luther

PRAYER IS *aligning* OURSELVES

WITH THE PURPOSES OF GOD.

— E. Stanley Jones

HOW IS GOD RESPONDING TO YOUR PRAYERS?

IN ALL MY PRAYERS FOR ALL OF YOU,

I ALWAYS *pray with joy*...
— PHILIPPIANS 1:4

HOW IS GOD RESPONDING TO YOUR PRAYERS?

NEVER WAS A FAITHFUL PRAYER LOST. SOME PRAYERS HAVE A LONGER VOYAGE THAN OTHERS, BUT THEN THEY RETURN WITH THEIR RICHER LADING AT LAST, SO THAT THE PRAYING SOUL IS A GAINER BY WAITING FOR AN ANSWER.

— William Gurnall

What are you P.U.S.H.ing for?

HOW IS GOD RESPONDING TO YOUR PRAYERS?

Just keep
PRAYING...
...until
SOMETHING
happens!